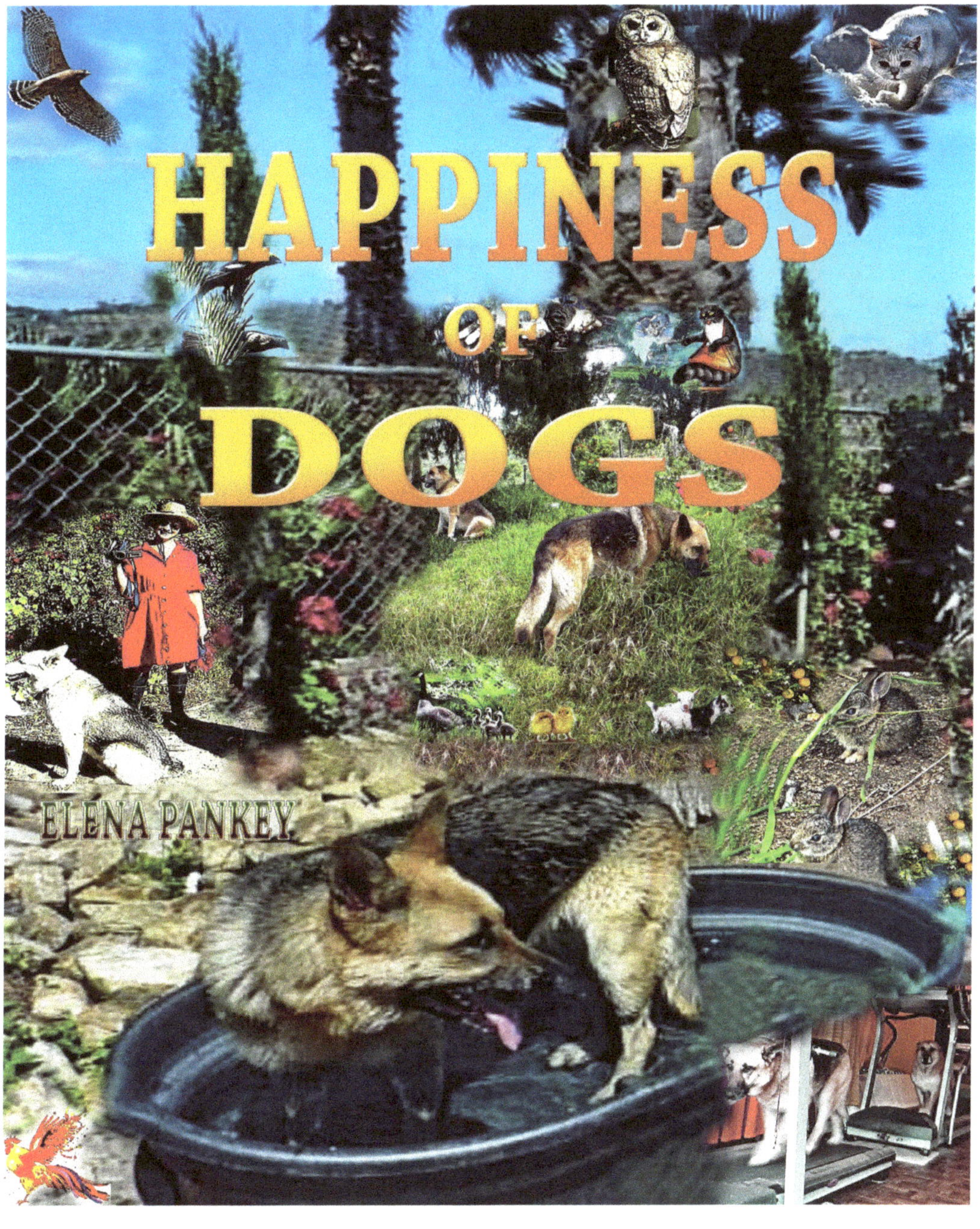

978-1-952907-48-7

I0379527

Happiness of the Dogs

Elena Pankey

No copyright infringement is intended
AllRightsReserved2021@ElenaPankey

***

Contents

About the Book	4
About the Author	5
Tuzik	6
Companionship	8
Porches	9
Good Life	11
Garden for All	14
Work is Happiness	15
For Parents	17
Proverbs	21
Rights Reserved	23
New Books	24

***

Treat your pets in a way as you want to be treated.

About the Book

This is a beautiful book for children, which tells about intelligent German Shepard dogs Tuzik and Sonia. They were lucky to live on a great ranch in California, loved their masters, and enjoyed their happy life. They had their own world and their own purpose which was in serving their master. They understood everything around them very well and spoke in their own language. They had their own deep feelings, loved the master with no conditions, and were infinitely devoted.

The dogs could tell many funny or sad stories about their lives if somebody would really listen to them.

We have to remember that when we tame dogs, we are forever responsible for them. Your loving dog will be your most devoted friend and will always be your joy in any conditions and sorrows.

About the Author

The author – Elena Pankey - has created many fascinating books in Russian and English which were published in Europe and America. Among them, it is worth noting several funny books about the life of cats and dogs, about monuments to beloved animals.

Her books about Argentine tango, about the famous Ukrainian artist Valeria Bulat, cannot be ignored. Particular attention should be paid to her historical and biographical trilogy about Gelendzhik. It is extremely interesting to read about her memories of this city and its people who lived there during 1950-1990.

The author has many years of experience in various fields of education, literature, theater, dance, cinematography. She especially enjoyed work as a guide in the palaces of Leningrad and traveling with tourists in the Baltic States. She also shared with people her love of art and knowledge of the beautiful museums of St. Petersburg.

During the years of "perestroika" she had her own successful business, which gave her the opportunity to travel around the world. Finally, she found her true happiness in California. There she opened her dance school, was the producer and performer, and organized some charity concerts. Then, she started to write her many books, published around the world.

***

Tuzik

Once upon a time, there were many different animals happily living at a California ranch. They knew that they had only one garden for all. So they lived together in peace and enjoyed good friendship.

Among them there was a smart dog, Tuzik, who lived in the front yard. His breed belonged to a very good and old line of German Shepherds. His main desire was to serve and protect people who owned him.

The ranch was on the top of the hill, far away from everything and from everybody.

The front yard and the garden were surrounded by a metal net fence. The dog Tuzik could freely run everywhere, but he did not have anybody to bark at or to play with. So, often he was just sad and lonely.

Only from time to time a car with a mail delivery would come to the ranch, and it was the happiest time for Tuzik. He could express his desire to work and to show his owner that he is a very useful dog. Since no strangers would come near the house, most of the time Tuzik was bored without barking and protecting something. He wanted to do his job guarding the property of the owners

His mistress Lila loved the smart German Shepard dogs, and especially she loved her dog Tuzik. She bought him a big dog house and many wonderful toys. Also Tuzik had a special bench with a mattress on the main porch near the house. But Tuzik was often lying in his comfortable house and did not want to play. He dreamed to have a friend.

Companionship

So, one day, the mistress understood that Tuzik was asking for a companion. She decided to bring home a new small puppy and named it Sonia.

First, when Sonia saw the big dog Tuzik, she was surprised about his size. But Tuzik had very kind eyes, and Sonia was not afraid of him.

Sometimes California's summer could be incredibly hot, especially on the paved front yard. On such very hot days, some other living creatures also tried to stay in the shade of the umbrellas or hide in the grass. Sometimes when the house door would be open for a minute, the wonderful coolness of the fans poured out onto the hot tiles of the sunny yard.

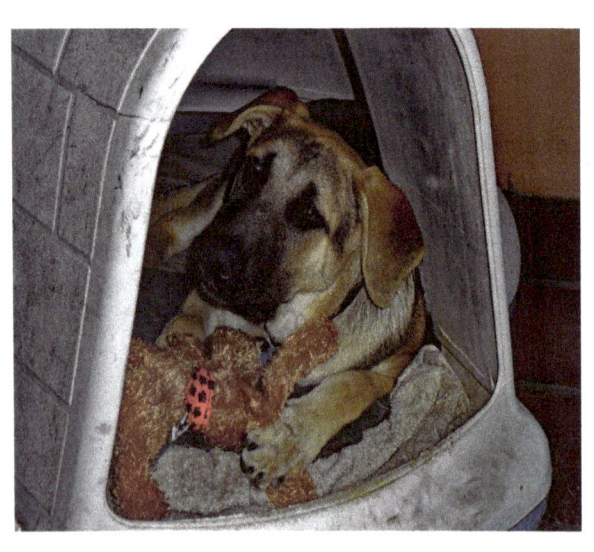

At that time, if dogs were not around, some mice could run into the ranch house and hide under the table.

After breakfast Tuzik tried to hide in the cool garage. And Sonia went to the garden to stay on the grass under the oak trees. Other times, most of the day they just were lying down on the steps of the stairway or on the patio and did not want even to move their ears.

Porches

There were two different porches on different side of the house. One porch was for Tuzik, and another porch was for Sonia. Each porch had several umbrellas. The dogs thought that it was relatively cool under the covers, as well, and often just laid down there.

The dogs of the German Shepard breed were very intelligent and observant. They knew many words and listened to the owner very attentively, trying to make them happy. If dogs could talk, they would tell many interesting stories. For example, often at night, Tuzik and Sonia saw the mice running around, and trying to steal some of the dogs food left after their meal. But the dogs did not want to hunt them, and continued just rest at the front yard until the morning.

Sometimes, the owners thought that the dogs were wagging their tails not for them personally, but for the meat they had in the hands. But these dogs were really loving and devoted creatures.

They just loved to do something for a reward. They felt that it had more meaning when they got a treat after they did something nice for the owner.

They always were looking at the people hands, thinking, what they might get for their effort to please them.

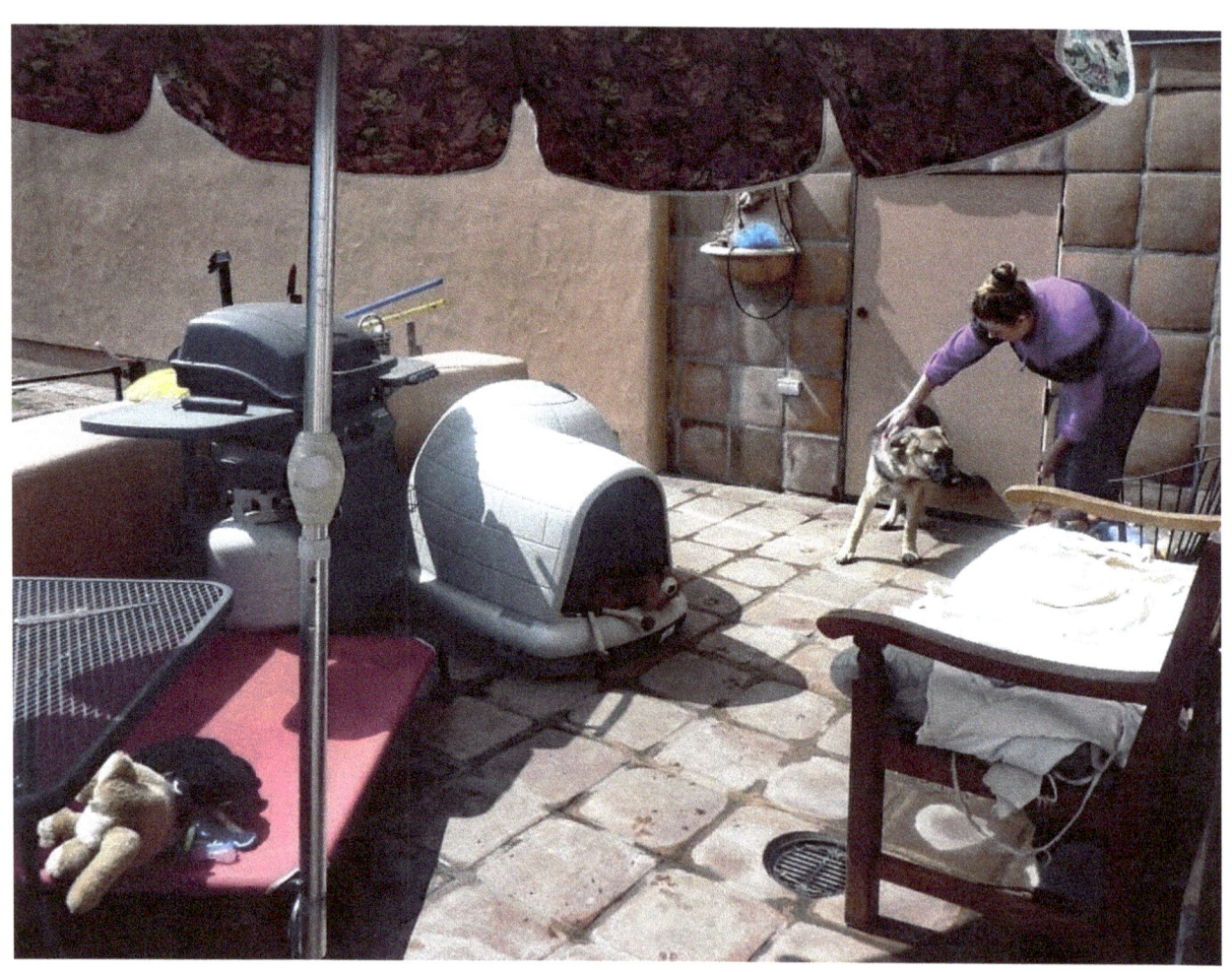

Good Life

The dog Tuzik had his personal house on the front yard. And the other dog Sonia had a big comfortable house at the back yard. So, they had their own territory to watch, guard and protect.

In addition, their loving mistress Alenushka got each of them a huge lounge and put it on the porch. Those lounges served dogs as wonderful resting places, as well, just for the variety of everyday life. With such wonderful care, the dogs felt lucky and good about their owners.

After the games, Tuzik and Sonia liked to rest in the hammock near the big people's pool. Also, they often enjoyed jumping in the big swimming pools to swim together with the owners.

Moreover, each dog had its own pool in the front yard to cool down on the sunny days. Especially, they wanted to swim after their exercises on the tread mills.

The tread mills were in the garage. Their mistress told them that exercise is good for the improvement of the muscles. Dogs did not want to argue about it, but they did not often want to do any exercise voluntarily. They were doing it only because after that they always got delicious dinner.

The dinner was near the pool during the sunset. Each dog had his own plate with some dry food or canned food. Their loving mistress put their plates on a special box so that the dogs would not bend over too much and would be more comfortable to eat.

Garden for All

Around the front yard, there was a special fence that the dogs would not run away  to the fruit orchards. Also, that fenced territory included a big hillside garden with different fruit trees, flowers, and bushes. The dogs knew that it was very useful for them to eat medicinal herbs that they easily found in the garden. But during some hot days dogs did not want to move without a very good reason. They knew that they will have a very good dinner, that their mistress provided them. So, they did not want to hunt neither rabbit nor squirrels in the garden.

There were a lot of rabbits and squirrels in the garden living under the bushes. At sunset, they came out from their hiding places to get some fresh green grass or fruits for dinner. They enjoyed the garden for themselves without fear of the hunting dogs.

***

Work is Happiness

The dogs worked a lot, loved it and had fun with it. Tuzik and Sonia loved to do something together with the owners. Having a job was fulfilling, and being busy gave them the meaning and joy in their lives. Sometimes, the owner put a backpack on the dogs and took them to the orchard to collect some fruits. They enjoyed any walk with people. But especially, they enjoyed the ride in the truck with the owner.

Sonia was very sociable and wanted to play all the time. She was sure that her friend must be Tuzik and he should play with her. However, Tuzik was very jealous that younger dog Sonia took all attention of his owners. But since the owners loved her, Tuzik decided to be tolerant of her, as well, and slowly became accustomed to the cheerful and playful girl Sonia.

Sonia generally thought that her existence was to make everybody happy. This is why she waved her tail, and kissed everybody. That was her nature.

The mistress Alenushka prohibited dogs to jump on her with any kisses or hugs. Then, Sonia learned that other owner, a nice man Victusha did not prohibit her from jumping

and kisses. So every time Sonia saw Victusha she jumped very high and kissed him. It was her way of saying; "*I love you the most because you never scold us for anything.*"

The dogs took every day as a new beginning; every day was a new day. They loved everything that was happening during the day. There was no moment that they ever could repeat. And it was their happiness.

***

For Parents

The cat and dog have long been the most popular pets. They are the most intelligent, easily trained and the most comfortable to live at home. In a cat people often see a reflection of the feminine features. And a dog is mostly a symbol and expression of male characteristics. Of course, it all depends on the size of a dog, its breed and who brings him up. Traditionally, the dog lived in a yard, acting as a watchdog. And the cat often lived in a house, creating more comfort and coziness.

As we noted, over time a cat and a dog adopt the features of their owners and became alike. However, it always depends on how much time the hosts spend with their pets, how attentive they are to the pets' needs. Moreover, animals are boundlessly devoted not only to

the house, but they become attached to the master and love him wholeheartedly.

They are always trying to please us as much as they can. Most importantly, they do not know the word "betrayal."

However, sometimes we see that people get a cat or a dog for their children mostly for an amusement. When the animals are small, people enjoy them as living toys. However, not many people think in advance how things will be when the pets grow up. Then, having played enough with a puppy or kitten, without having taught them good manners, people might heartlessly throw pets to the mercy of fate, without thinking about the suffering of the animal.

In good families, pets become family members, and adults teach their children to understand that their pets have their own feelings and simple thoughts. Parents emphasize how important it is to care for the pets, to communicate with and love them, as people should love each other. It is pet care that brings up the best qualities in a person. And it is the best to start doing this from childhood.

Later on, it is clear that the attitude towards animals is a person's character. We treat animals in the same way as we relate to other people: as attentively, with love and care, as our soul lets us or we are able to. How much time and effort a person gives to a cat or dog, in the same way he would act in the human relationship. Attention and treatments of animals is like a litmus test of human characteristics.

***

Proverbs

An honest man is not the worse because a dog barks at him.

***

If you stop every time a dog barks, your road will never end.

***

Dog does not eat dog.

***

Give a dog a bad name and hang him.

***

Why keep a dog and bark yourself?

***

Every dog is allowed one bite.

***

A good dog deserves a good bone.

***

To live long, eat like a cat, drink like a dog.

***

The barking of a dog does not disturb the man on a camel.

***

Children aren't dogs; adults aren't gods.

***

Beware of a silent dog and still water.

***

One dog barks at something, the rest bark at him.

***

Do not respond to a barking dog.

***

Only mad dogs and Englishmen go out in the noonday sun.

***

Those who sleep with dogs will rise with fleas.

***

Show a dog a finger, and he wants the whole hand.

Rights Reserved

All rights reserved. No part of this publication may be reproduced, distributed, or transmitted in any form or by any means, including photocopying, recording, or other electronic or mechanical methods, without the prior written permission of the publisher, unless brief quotations are made.

The title of the book is published in the United States of America.

The first edition was in 2021. Photos, drawings created, redone by Elena Bulat.

***

New Books

No copyright infringement is intended

AllRightsReserved2021@ElenaPankey

www.ingramcontent.com/pod-product-compliance
Lightning Source LLC
Chambersburg PA
CBHW042016120526
44592CB00044B/2995